CHEBET
and the Lost Goat

Ben Alex

Photographs by
Ben Alex and Ray Davis

A LION BOOK
Tring · Batavia · Sydney

4

'Raiders!' Chebet shouted from the top of her tall tree half-way up the hillside of the Amaya Valley. She pointed to the slopes above.

Chebet knew the dangers in the bush country and she feared the cattle raiders most of all. They were bandits from the Turkana tribe who would sneak down and steal cattle from the Pokot people, her people.

There were other dangers too—lions, leopards, hyenas and crocodiles. Only yesterday, the men living close to the river had found a giant python backed into its hole in the river bank with a dead goat kid in its mouth. Chebet trembled as she thought about it.

Then her brother Diyele joined Chebet in the tree. 'Oh, you dummy!' he said. 'It's only a troop of baboons.'

Chebet didn't like being called 'dummy', but she was relieved to be wrong. They stayed to watch the baboons play before going home.

Below them lay the Amaya Valley. Because it is on the equator it is warm and sunny all year round, and the sun shines directly overhead. There are usually two rainy seasons each year, but sometimes the rain doesn't come. Then the trees and grass shrivel and dry up, the crops cannot grow, and the animals become very thirsty.

6

'Chebet!' a shout came from below. 'Toto has disappeared!'

Chebet hurried down from the tree and ran as fast as her feet could carry her down the rocky trail. 'Where can Toto have gone?' she wondered. In the distance she could see her family's mud hut surrounded by the dusty, dry bush country.

Chebet lived with her parents, her grandmother, and her brothers in a little round hut that her mother had made out of branches and clay. There was a fireplace in the middle of floor, and the roof was covered with grass.

As Chebet ran down the hillside, the goats grazing nearby stared after her. 'Baaa!' they called. But Chebet did not turn around. She even ran right past her father who was finishing his work in the cornfield.

Chebet's father was proud of this fine field that produced enough food for his large family and some to sell as well. Chebet and her brothers had grown up on a diet of milk, field corn and brown beans. Sometimes there had been some garden spinach, when the insects did not eat it all first. On special days there might be a piece of goat meat for supper.

Chebet knew she was nearly home when she reached the place where the cows always gathered in the late afternoon. The cows were big and lazy. They had humps on the back of their necks which acted as storage for water during the dry season. Chebet's father owned more than twenty cows and a plot of land in the highlands where it was not as dry as in the valley. The land he owned was called a *shamba*.

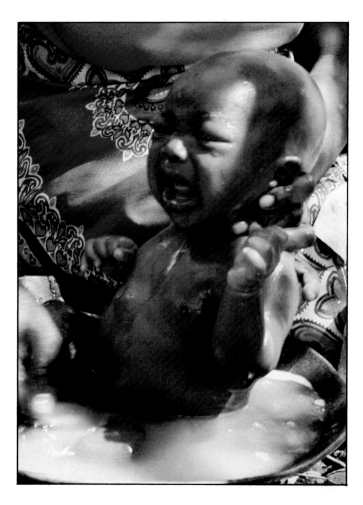

Eight years ago, when Chebet was born, the Amaya Valley had been green and leafy, not dry and dusty. It had rained a great deal that year and there was plenty to eat. Even the goats and the cows had eaten so much grass they were eager to be milked at the end of the day. Chebet was often bathed in a basin since there had been water to spare.

Chebet didn't have any toys to play with. But one day her father gave her a little golden chick. 'Chebet, this is your very own chick,' he had explained. 'Take good care of it. When it becomes a hen, you will get seven more chicks. Sell them and buy a goat kid. When the goat grows up, you will get seven more goat kids. Sell them and buy a calf. When the calf grows and starts to give milk, you will be rich!'

Chebet did take very good care of the chick, just as her father had told her to. The chick became a hen. Chebet sold the hen and its small chickens. Now she had a goat kid of her very own. And his name was Toto!

Sometimes Toto would sneak up behind Chebet and give her a soft butt on her bottom. Then he would leap away because he knew Chebet would come running after him. When they were tired of playing, Chebet and Toto often collapsed in the shade of a tree and fell asleep close together.

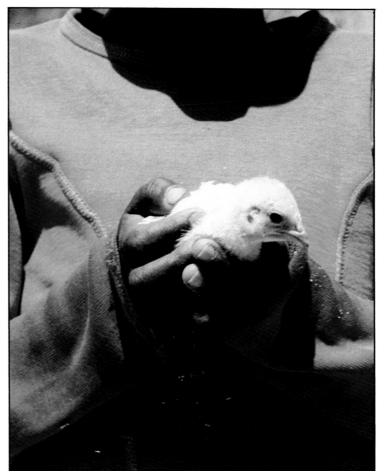

'Has Toto really disappeared?' Chebet gasped as she ran around the mud hut to the goat pen. 'No! No!' she cried. The other baby goats stared back at her. But Toto was not there.

Mother was gathering in the dry clothes. 'Chebet, we can only pray that Toto has not been hurt. Maybe he will wander home again by himself. It is too late to go looking now, and tomorrow there will be work to get done before school.'

When the boys arrived home everyone gathered to help make *ugali*, a cornmeal dough prepared twice a day for supper and breakfast. While they worked, they talked about Toto. Their mother told them the story they loved to hear about the time God had answered their prayers when Chebet was very ill.

'Most of our neighbours said that God was angry with us. They told us to sacrifice a goat kid to *Tororot* and to the spirits of our dead grandparents,' she said. 'They warned us if we did not honour these spirits, Chebet would most certainly die. Our neighbours did not know that *Tororot* is a loving, Father God.'

There are 200,000 Pokot people in western Kenya. Most of these people believe in one God, whom they call *Tororot*. They believe he lives on the highest mountain-top above the Amaya Valley. But there are a group of Pokots who have learned that God revealed himself to us through his Son Jesus Christ. They have learned to trust in Jesus instead of fearing God or the spirits of their dead ancestors. When Chebet's mother became a Christian, she sold her traditional Pokot costumes of beads and goatskins. She wanted to show her life had changed.

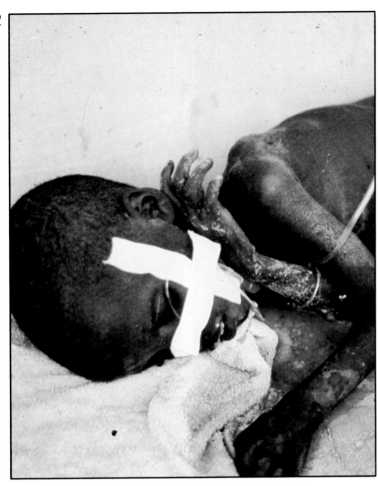

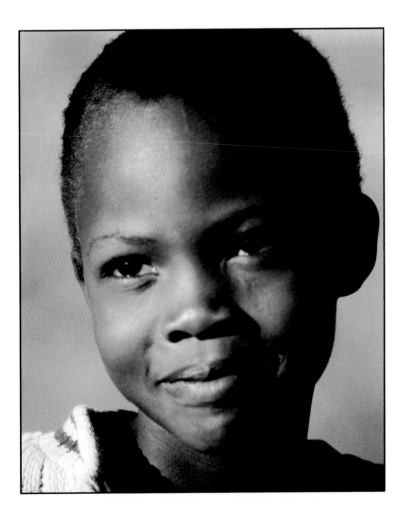

That time when Chebet had been very ill and close to death, her mother and father had made a daring decision. Instead of sacrificing to the spirits of the dead, they had decided to pray to Jesus and to wait for his answer. They knew very well that in their country one out of every two children will die before the age of five years. Yet they had prayed earnestly and waited. They met with other believers in the little church hut of palm branches to pray for Chebet and to worship.

When Chebet did get well again, the entire Amaya Valley had heard about it! Chebet's father had told everyone he met, 'Jesus Christ is the true Son of God!' After Chebet was healed he started to tell the Pokot people the Good News about Jesus.

Chebet's mother told her children, 'My heart was so happy I cried tears of joy!'

That evening, as the family gathered inside the hut, everyone was quieter than usual. Chebet did not say a word. As the sun set she stood in the doorway thinking about Toto and about *Tororot* and about his Son Jesus. Chebet wanted to believe that her mother and father were right. She wanted to believe in Jesus.

Chebet looked to the horizon. It had always seemed like a welcoming doorstep to the world outside the valley. And as Chebet thought about Toto lost out there somewhere, she wished she had wings to fly to the end of the earth to be able to find him. In the distance she saw vultures circling low in the sky.

Early the next morning, Chebet rolled up the goatskins from the floor around the fire where her family had slept. She swept the floor clean and fed the chickens so they would not peck around inside, looking for food.

Mother sent her off to fetch water from the pond below the dam, before other people got there and it muddied. Then she would have to gather the day's supply of firewood.

Chebet set off down the trail. She was in a hurry because she wanted to have time to look for Toto, too. Along the way, Chebet met other women also on their way to get water. She asked everyone she passed, 'Have you seen a pure white baby goat?'

They laughed at her. 'A goat kid won't live long on its own out here. Forget about it and go home.'

But Chebet could not forget about Toto. At the pond, Chebet looked down and saw a lion lying quietly by the edge, enjoying the last moments of the cool of the day. The lion reminded Chebet of the danger Toto might be in. Or was it already too late? She waited in the bush until the lion left, then took her water and hurried back home with it.

Already, the day was getting hot. Chebet did not have to go far from home to gather wood. All the time, her thoughts were on Toto. She could not bear to think of letting a day go by without finding him.

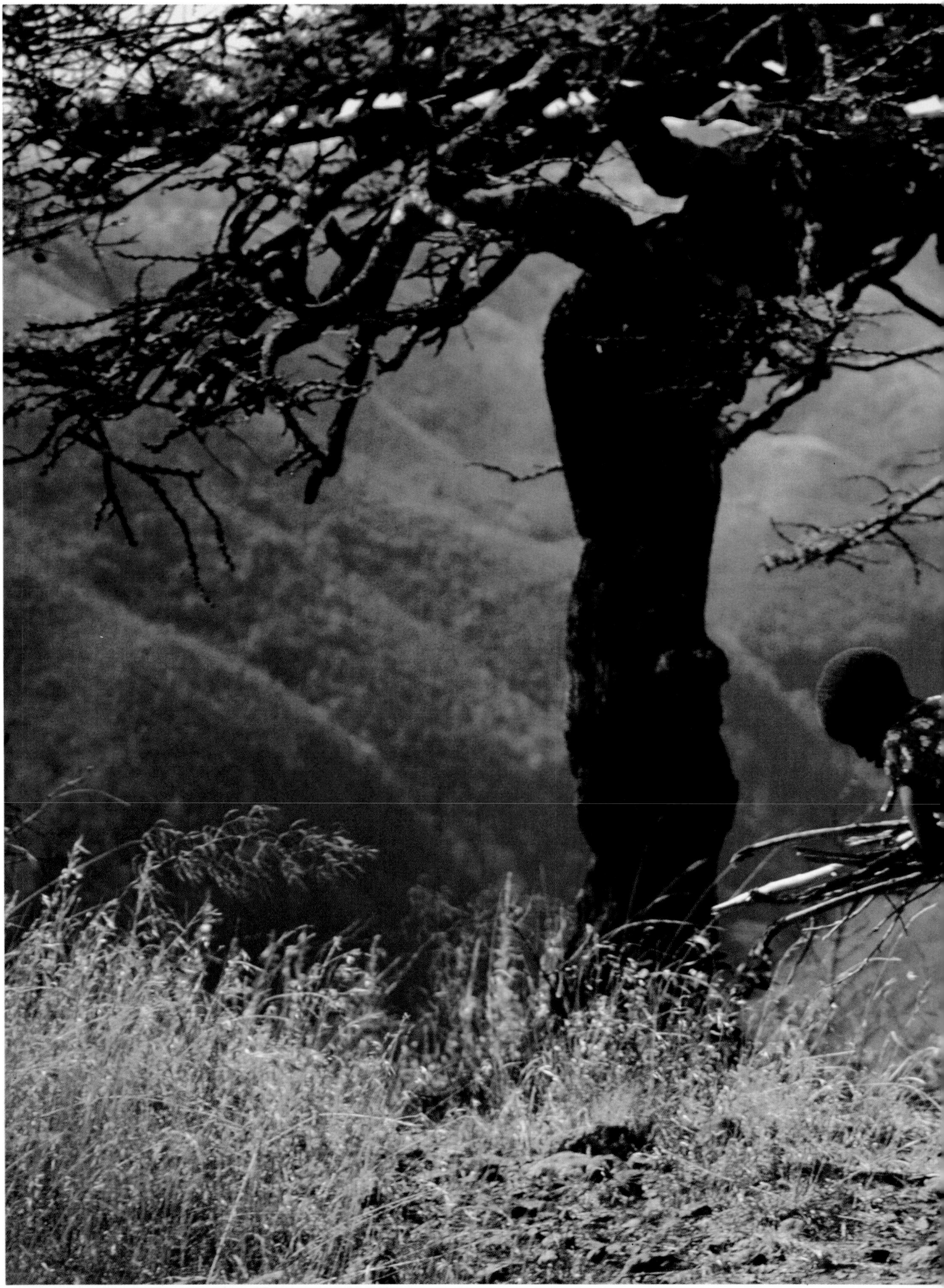

On her way home with the wood needed for that day's cooking, Chebet went around to the neighbouring huts. At each one, she met the curious gazes of children and animals. 'Have you seen a pure white baby goat?' she asked.

The children just looked at Chebet. Sometimes she peered into their huts or goat pens. But she did not find Toto. And it seemed as if no one else cared if she found him or not.

Chebet left the firewood outside her own hut and quickly headed up into the dry hills. She was determined not to go home again without Toto. She walked and walked, past the river and further than she had ever been before. The narrow trails were dusty and rocky. Now and then a scorpion scuttled across the earth in front of her toes and crawled under a large stone.

Chebet passed the big dam a long way up the river. The dam had been built to catch the precious water coming from the hills and mountains in a reservoir to irrigate the Amaya Valley. Further along, Chebet knew she would come to a small lake—and even further, to the jungle. But she did not care how far she would have to go to find her baby goat.

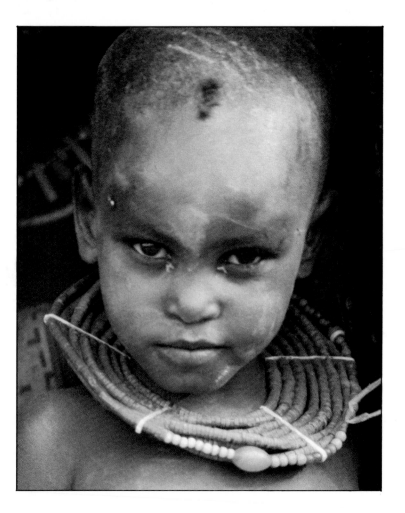

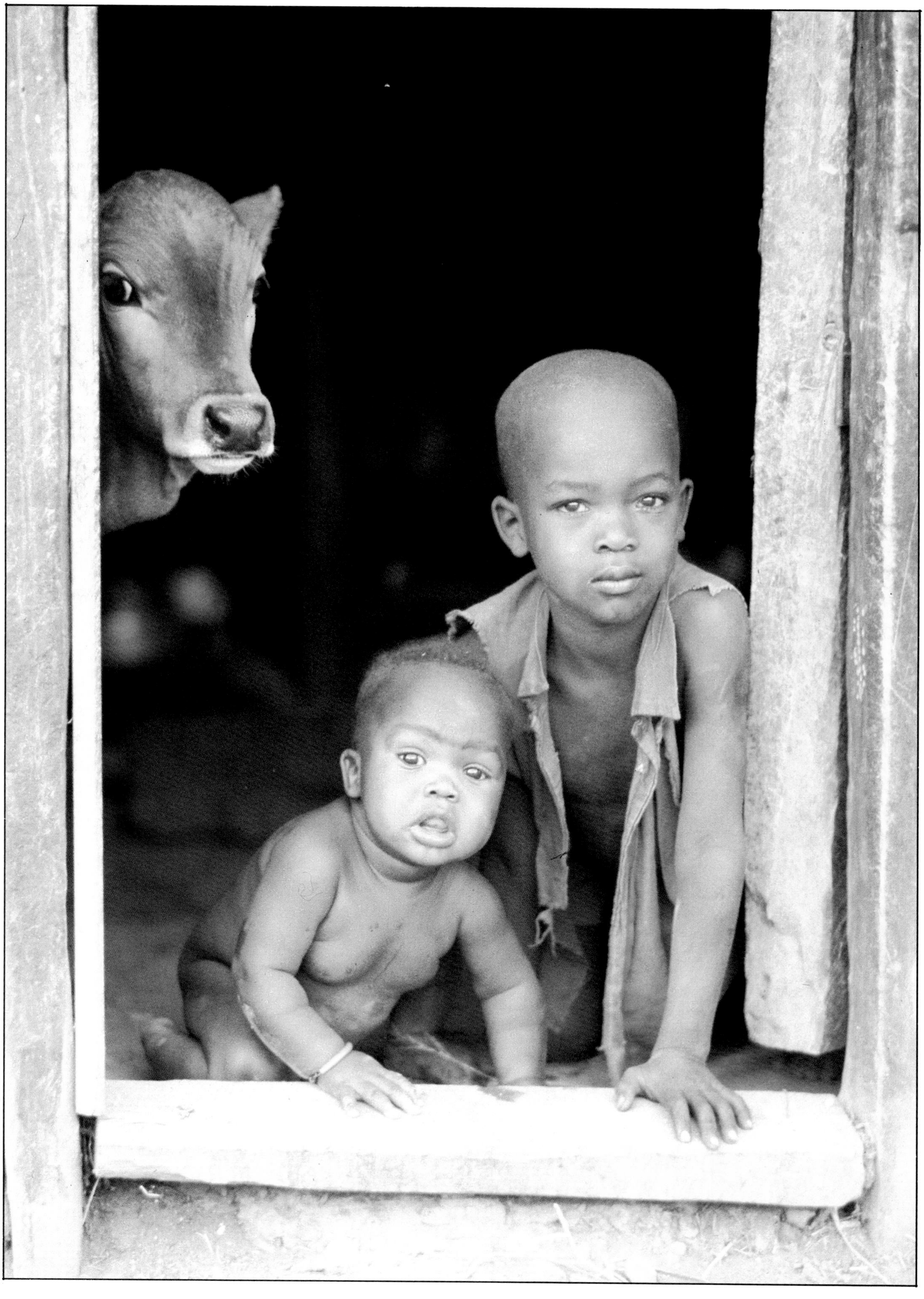

Far along the trail, between the lake and the jungle, Chebet met a woman who offered to help her find Toto. 'Come with me!' said the woman. Her ears were decorated with large golden rings.

Suddenly, a boy appeared out of nowhere and pointed a bow and arrow right at Chebet. Chebet was not sure she wanted to follow one step further.

Just then, the sound of chanting and musical instruments filled the air. Chebet looked in the direction the woman was taking her. She saw a group of men dancing in a circle. 'We are dancing for the spirits of the dead,' said the woman. 'These spirits can help you if you join us.'

Two men walked by carrying a dead goat kid. They were going to sacrifice it to the evil spirits. Chebet stopped in her tracks. 'Supposing that was Toto?' she thought.

People who worship and pray to the spirits of the dead believe they must offer the best they have to win protection from danger and the favour of the spirits. They believe these spirits live all around them in the trees, the rocks, in animals, and in the darkness.

Chebet turned and ran down the hill the same way she had come. She did not stop until she reached the river bed.

By this time Chebet saw that other Pokot children were on their way to school. 'I should be in school, too,' thought Chebet. 'And maybe some of the others have seen Toto. Or maybe Toto is waiting for me there!'

Chebet headed for school even though she did not have her uniform on. Like most other children from the valley, Chebet did not go to school every day. When there was work to be done at home, she stayed with her mother. Sometimes, the teacher did not show up anyway. Learning to read and write was a slow process.

'What can you tell me about *Mzee*?' asked the teacher.

Chebet did not care about *Mzee* today. She could think only of Toto, her very best friend.

'Chebet?' asked the teacher.

Chebet knew the answer well. Everyone in Kenya knew about *Mzee*, the great old man. '*Mzee* was Jomo Kenyatta, the first president of Kenya in 1963, the year of *Uhuru*.'

'And what can you tell me about the year of *Uhuru*?' interrupted the teacher.

Chebet recited, '*Uhuru* is the year of freedom when Kenya became independent of British rule and got its own flag with three stripes: black, green, red.'

After school, Chebet hurried off before her brothers could ask her any questions. She wandered through the bush to check other goat pens and huts in the village.

One of the last huts Chebet came to was where her friend Chepsanyak lived. Chebet was on the verge of tears when Chepsanyak came out to meet her.

'*Karam!* Hello!' said Chepsanyak. 'Come in. You look tired and hungry.' But Chepsanyak sensed that Chebet needed someone to talk to more than anything else.

Chebet blurted, 'I've given up hope of finding my little goat kid, Toto. I've looked everywhere.'

Chebet knew her friend would understand. Though Chepsanyak was only sixteen years old, she was courageous and wise. When she was thirteen, Chepsanyak's father had sold her in marriage to an old man who offered a high price for her. But Chepsanyak had heard that this man had often beaten his first wife, who had run away from him. So before the wedding could take place, Chepsanyak had run away with a young man, Nyoru, who loved her. Now the two of them were happily married and the marriage was accepted even by Chepsanyak's father.

'Chebet!' said Chepsanyak. 'Let me tell you something that helped me when I was sad and afraid, the time my first baby died. I was all alone, for no Pokot will come near a woman whose child has died. My husband's mother left food outside my door. But I could not eat. I felt like the only woman in the whole world who ever lost a baby. Then your mother came to me. She was not afraid of what others might think. She told me she had lost a baby too. She read to me from the Bible, the Word of God. I was comforted. I could eat. I put the words in my heart.'

By the time Chebet left her friend's hut it was nearly sundown. As she started up the long trail that led back to her home, she knew that if she did not find Toto soon it would be too late.

Suddenly, she heard a faint bleating sound not too far away. Chebet leapt upon a rock and looked around. Once again she heard the faint sound. 'Baaa! Baaa!' Was it just the goats on the hillside, or could it be . . . ?

Chebet crept further into the underbrush. Her father had sternly warned her never to go off the trail. 'I'd better not go any further,' she thought.

Then something rustled in one of the dry trees above her. Chebet caught sight of a leopard lying on a thick branch. Fortunately, the leopard looked satisfied and lazy. But it was keeping an eye on something below. When it saw Chebet coming, it jumped to the ground and disappeared.

'Baaa!' The bleating sound was louder. And there in a crevice below her, Chebet saw a pure white goat kid wedged between two jagged rocks, unable to free itself.

'Toto!' screamed Chebet. Before she had a chance to think about the danger she was in, she jumped down and grabbed the goat. Then she scurried out onto the trail again.

In the distance, Chebet heard a sound that made her blood run cold, a sound she knew well enough. Goose-pimples prickled her arms. It was the cattle raiders!

Chebet clasped Toto closely and crept behind a large boulder on the other side of the trail. 'Dear God,' she prayed, 'keep Toto quiet. Don't let him make a sound.'

Chebet waited and watched as the cattle raiders passed close by her. Then she ran all the way home with Toto in her arms.

Back home, Chebet's family had stopped worrying about Toto and started worrying about Chebet instead. Her father had set out to look for her while her brother Diyele had his eyes glued on the trail leading up to their hut. 'There she is!' he yelled.

'Chebet! You naughty little girl!' cried Mother as she ran down the trail and squeezed Chebet tight. But Chebet did not mind being scolded. She knew Mother was happy she was home again. And Chebet was happy, too.

Chebet told her family about all the people she had met: the curious children, the woman who looked at her strangely but had offered to help, the boy with the bow and arrow, the men dancing ritual dances for the spirits of the dead and their sacrifice, the dead goat she had thought at first was Toto. As they sat on the floor around the fire, the flickering flames carved out funny shadow-expressions on their faces. When Chebet told about the leopard in the tree above her and the Turkana cattle raiders, everybody held their breath.

Then Chebet's father took out his most precious possession, a New Testament in his own language. He read the story from the Gospel of Matthew, 'If a man has a hundred sheep, and one wanders away and is lost, what will he do? Won't he leave the ninety-nine others and go out into the hills to search for the lost one? And if he finds it, he will rejoice over it more than over the ninety-nine others safe at home! Just so, it is not my Father's will that even one of these little ones should perish.'

At bedtime, Chebet could not get to sleep. She went outside and sat on a rock in the moonlight. The stars were very big and they sparkled brightly. Chebet got up and quietly went out in the moonlight to the goat pen. She took Toto in her arms. 'You naughty little goat!' she said over and over.

The wind drifted over the hills and rattled the tin buckets hanging outside the huts. Far away a dog barked and a mother sang softly to her child. The crickets sang in the trees. Chebet closed the gate to the goat pen very securely. Toto nestled up among the other sleepy little goats. Chebet was happy she had not asked for the help of the spirits of the dead, nor given up searching for Toto. She knew *Tororot*, the true God, had helped her to find Toto and that he had protected her own life, just like the lost sheep in the Bible story.

Before she fell asleep, Chebet whispered, 'All is well, good, sweet.'